15-Minute Foodie

Holiday Recipes in 15 Minutes or Less

by Tamara JM Peterson

CAPSTONE PRESS
a capstone imprint

Dabble Lab is published by Capstone Press, an imprint of Capstone.
1710 Roe Crest Drive, North Mankato, Minnesota 56003
capstonepub.com

Library of Congress Cataloging-in-Publication Data
Names: Peterson, Tamara JM, author.
Title: Holiday recipes in 15 minutes or less / by Tamara JM Peterson.
Description: North Mankato, Minnesota : Capstone Press, a Capstone imprint, [2024] | Series: 15-minute foodie | Includes bibliographical references. | Audience: Ages 8-11 | Audience: Grades 4-6 | Summary: "Looking to celebrate the holidays with quick and delicious recipes? Become a 15-minute foodie! Mix up a batch of rich, spiced Mexican hot chocolate to honor Día de los Muertos. Assemble a cute marshmallow puffed rice turkey to celebrate Thanksgiving. Make latkes out of hash browns to commemorate Hanukkah. These quick, fun, yummy recipes will be ready to eat in 15 minutes or less"— Provided by publisher.
Identifiers: LCCN 2023024196 (print) | LCCN 2023024197 (ebook) | ISBN 9781669061656 (hardcover) | ISBN 9781669061618 (pdf) | ISBN 9781669061632 (kindle edition) | ISBN 9781669061625 (epub)
Subjects: LCSH: Holiday cooking—Juvenile literature. | Quick and easy cooking—Juvenile literature. | LCGFT: Cookbooks
Classification: LCC TX739 .P46 2024 (print) | LCC TX739 (ebook) | DDC 641.5/68—dc23/eng/20230524
LC record available at https://lccn.loc.gov/2023024196
LC ebook record available at https://lccn.loc.gov/2023024197

Image Credits
Adobe Stock: bonchan, 18 (bowl), Monkey Business, 5, pololia, 4; iStockphoto: bassey edoho, 18 (rice); Mighty Media, Inc.: project photos; Shutterstock: Rohan Divetiya, 10 (cloth)

Design Elements
iStockphoto: Sirintra_Pumsopa, yugoro; Mighty Media, Inc.

Editorial Credits
Editor: Jessica Rusick
Designers: Sarah DeYoung and Denise Hamernik
Cooks: Tamara JM Peterson and Chelsey Luciow

Content Consultants
Christina Gish Hill, Professor of American Indian Studies, Iowa State University
Frederick Douglass Opie, Professor of History and Foodways, Babson College
Deven Patel, Professor of South Asia Studies, University of Pennsylvania
Mun'im Sirry, Professor of Theology, University of Notre Dame

Printed and bound in China. 5593

Table of Contents

Holiday Recipes in Fifteen! 4
Ham & Pickle Roll 6
Chocolate-Covered Pretzels 8
Rava Kesari 10
Hash Brown Latkes 12
Easter Egg Bunnies 14
Mexican Hot Chocolate 16
Jollof Rice 18
U.S. Flag Cookie 20
Three Sisters Salad 22
Spooky Pumpkins 24
Crisped Rice Turkeys 26
Reindeer Poop 28
Spiced Meat Rolls 30
Read More 32
Internet Sites 32
About the Author 32

Holiday Recipes in Fifteen!

Are you looking for recipes to celebrate holidays from around the world? Whether you're making crisped rice turkeys for Thanksgiving, hash brown latkes for Hanukkah, or a spiced meat roll for Eid al-Fitr, this book is full of ideas to celebrate in style. And the best part is, these recipes come together in 15 minutes or less! So grab your kitchen supplies and read through the tips on the next page. Soon enough, you'll be a 15-minute foodie!

Basic Supplies

baking sheet
blender
frying pan
knife and cutting board
measuring cups and spoons
mixing bowls
saucepan
spatula
strainer
toothpicks

Kitchen Tips

Ask an adult for permission before you make a recipe.

Read through the recipe and set out all ingredients and supplies before you start cooking.

Using metric tools? Use the conversion chart below to make your recipe measure up.

Wash your hands before and after you handle food. Wash and dry fresh produce before use.

Ask an adult for help when using a knife, blender, or stovetop. Wear oven mitts when removing items from the oven or microwave.

When you are done making food, clean your work surface. Wash dirty dishes and put all supplies and ingredients back where you found them.

Standard	Metric
¼ teaspoon	1.25 grams or milliliters
½ teaspoon	2.5 g or mL
1 teaspoon	5 g or mL
1 tablespoon	15 g or mL
¼ cup	57 g (dry) or 60 mL (liquid)
⅓ cup	75 g (dry) or 80 mL (liquid)
½ cup	114 g (dry) or 125 mL (liquid)
⅔ cup	150 g (dry) or 160 mL (liquid)
¾ cup	170 g (dry) or 175 mL (liquid)
1 cup	227 g (dry) or 240 mL (liquid)
1 quart	950 mL

Ham & Pickle Roll

New Year's Eve on the Gregorian calendar is the last day of the year. Many people celebrate by hosting parties with snacks and appetizers! For a quick New Year's Eve appetizer, try this classic pickle roll.

Ingredients

4 flour tortillas
8 tablespoons spreadable cream cheese
8 ham slices
1 jar baby dill pickles

Supplies

measuring spoons
spatula
toothpicks
knife and cutting board

1. Spread 2 tablespoons cream cheese on each tortilla.

2. Top each tortilla with two ham slices.
3. Place a row of pickles across the tortilla and roll tightly.

4. Insert toothpicks into the roll about every 1 to 2 inches (2.5 to 5 centimeters).
5. Slice between the toothpicks and serve!

Food Tip

Use garden vegetable cream cheese or garlic cream cheese to give your rolls extra flavor!

Chocolate-Covered Pretzels

Valentine's Day celebrates love and friendship. Whip up a batch of sweet and savory chocolate-covered pretzels to give to your valentine!

Ingredients

1 bag pretzel rods
½ cup white chocolate chips
1 tablespoon vegetable oil
sprinkles (red, pink)

Supplies

parchment paper
baking sheet
measuring cups and spoons
microwave-safe bowl
spoon

1. Spread out the pretzel rods on the parchment-lined baking sheet.
2. Place the white chocolate chips and oil in the microwave-safe bowl. Microwave them in 20-second intervals, stirring between each one, until the chocolate is melted and smooth.
3. Use the spoon to drizzle the chocolate over the pretzels.
4. Decorate the pretzels with sprinkles.

5. Place the baking sheet in the refrigerator for 10 minutes or until the chocolate hardens. Share your pretzels with friends and family!

Food Tip

Experiment with your pretzel rod designs! Stir food coloring into white chocolate for a new drizzle color. Or use different varieties of sprinkles!

Rava Kesari

Diwali is an Indian holiday representing the triumph of light over darkness. It is also called the Festival of Lights. Diwali celebrations feature fireworks and feasts! Celebrate Diwali in style by making rava kesari, a sweet dish from southern India.

Ingredients

1½ cups water
¼ cup ghee or butter, plus extra
9 cashews (8 halved, 1 whole)
½ cup rava (also called semolina)
1 cup sugar
yellow food coloring
¼ teaspoon cardamom

Supplies

knife and cutting board
measuring cups and spoons
saucepan
frying pan
spatula
spoon
ladle
bowl
serving plate

1. Bring the water to a boil in the saucepan.

2. While the water boils, heat the ghee or butter in the frying pan over medium heat. Add the cashews and cook them until they are golden. Then remove the cashews from the pan and set them aside. Leave the ghee or butter in the pan.

3. Add the rava to the same pan. Stir constantly until you can smell it.

4. Slowly ladle the boiling water from step 1 into the frying pan, stirring constantly.

5. Once all the water is added, add the sugar and food coloring. Stir the mixture for four minutes.

6. Sprinkle the cardamom and cashew halves into the pan.

7. Spread ghee or butter on the bottom and sides of the bowl. Spoon the rava kesari into it. Push the rava kesari down with the spatula to make sure it sticks together.

8. Flip the rava kesari onto the plate. Serve it with the whole cashew on top!

Hash Brown Latkes

Hanukkah is an eight-day Jewish holiday. It lasts for this long to commemorate an ancient miracle during which holy oil that should have lasted for only one day burned for eight days. Oily foods such as latkes (LOT-kahs) are traditionally eaten during Hanukkah. Make your own hash brown latkes to celebrate!

Ingredients

4 cups frozen hash browns, thawed
2 large eggs
salt to taste
2 to 4 cups vegetable oil
applesauce (optional)
sour cream (optional)

Supplies

measuring cups and spoons
strainer
cold water
paper towels
large mixing bowl
frying pan
spatula
plate

1. Strain and rinse the hash browns with water. Press on the hash browns with paper towels to squeeze out as much water as possible.
2. Mix the eggs, salt, and hash browns in the large mixing bowl.
3. Heat about ½ inch (1.3 cm) oil in the frying pan on medium-high heat.
4. When the oil is hot, scoop ¼ cups of the hash brown mixture into the pan.

5. Flatten the latkes with the spatula. Turn the heat to medium low.
6. Check the undersides of the latkes after about four minutes. Flip the latkes when the undersides are golden brown.
7. Let the latkes cook for another four minutes or until both sides are golden brown.
8. Place the latkes on a plate covered in paper towels to soak up excess oil. If you'd like, serve the latkes with applesauce or sour cream on the side!

Easter Egg Bunnies

Easter is a Christian holiday celebrating the resurrection of Jesus Christ. Many Easter celebrations feature symbols of renewal and newness. These include baby bunnies and eggs! Make a cute and shareable appetizer to celebrate Easter.

Ingredients

6 hard-boiled eggs, shelled
3 tablespoons mayonnaise
1 teaspoon Dijon mustard
⅛ teaspoon salt
¼ cup carrots
¼ cup black olives
¼ cup red bell pepper
2 stalks chives

Supplies

knife and cutting board
spoon
mixing bowl
fork
measuring cups and spoons
serving platter

1. Cut each egg in half lengthwise and carefully scoop the yolks into the mixing bowl. Set the egg whites aside to use as cups.

2. Smash the yolks with the fork. Then stir in the mayonnaise, mustard, and salt.

3. Scoop the egg yolk filling into the egg white cups.

4. Slice the carrots into 24 bunny-ear shapes. Place two on each egg.

5. Cut the olives into 24 tiny pieces for eyes. Cut the pepper into 12 tiny pieces for noses. Place the eyes and noses on the bunnies.

6. Slice the chives into thin strips and place them on the sides of the noses for whiskers.

7. Serve your cute Easter bunny eggs on a platter at Easter!

Mexican Hot Chocolate

Día de los Muertos is a traditional Mexican holiday honoring loved ones who have passed away. Many celebrations include Mexican hot chocolate! This rich, spiced drink is meant to entice the spirits of loved ones to return home.

Ingredients

2 cups milk
2 tablespoons unsweetened cocoa powder
2 tablespoons sugar
½ teaspoon cinnamon
⅛ teaspoon chili powder
¼ teaspoon vanilla
¼ cup bittersweet chocolate chips
mini marshmallows (optional)
chocolate sprinkles (optional)
cinnamon stick (optional)

Supplies

measuring cups and spoons
saucepan
whisk
mug

1. Warm the milk, cocoa powder, sugar, cinnamon, and chili powder in the saucepan on medium-high heat. Whisk the mixture together. Do not let it bubble.

2. Add the vanilla and chocolate chips to the saucepan. Continue whisking until the chocolate is melted.

3. Serve your delicious drink in your favorite mug! If you'd like, top it with marshmallows, sprinkles, or a cinnamon stick.

Food Tip

For a spicier drink, add ½ teaspoon cayenne pepper.

Jollof Rice

Juneteenth commemorates the end of slavery in the U.S. It is also a celebration of African American heritage. Red food is an important part of the celebration because red symbolizes the hardships enslaved people had to endure. The color also honors traditional West African dishes. Celebrate Juneteenth with jollof rice, a traditional red rice dish from West Africa.

Ingredients

1½ yellow onions, diced
1 tablespoon jarred minced ginger
⅓ cup vegetable oil
6-ounce can green chilis, diced
14-ounce can tomato sauce
6-ounce can tomato paste
3 cups precooked rice
2 teaspoons garlic powder
salt and pepper to taste
1 cup frozen peas and/or corn
1 stalk green onion, chopped (optional)

Supplies

knife and cutting board
measuring cups and spoons
blender
large, deep pan with lid
large spoon

1. Blend the onions, ginger, vegetable oil, and green chilis into a smooth paste.
2. Pour the mixture into the pan. Stir in the tomato sauce and tomato paste.
3. Cook the mixture over medium heat for five minutes.
4. Add the rice, garlic powder, and salt and pepper to the pan. Mix well.
5. Turn the heat to low and stir in the frozen vegetables.
6. Cover the pan and let the rice simmer for seven minutes, or until the frozen vegetables are warmed through. Top the rice with green onion if you'd like. Then dig in!

U.S. Flag Cookie

Celebrate U.S. independence with an easy and fun treat that's fancy enough to bring to any Fourth of July party.

Ingredients

4 large graham crackers
16-ounce can vanilla frosting
¼ cup blueberries
1 banana, cut into strips
½ cup raspberries

Supplies

knife and cutting board
spatula
measuring cups
serving plate

1. Lay the graham crackers side by side to make a rectangle. This is the flag.

2. Spread frosting on the flag.

3. Make red and white stripes across the flag with the bananas and raspberries. Leave a rectangular space at the top left of the flag open.
4. Decorate the top left of the flag with blueberries. Leave gaps between them to represent the flag's white stars.
5. Serve your sweet and patriotic creation on the serving plate!

Three Sisters Salad

Indigenous Peoples' Day is a U.S. holiday that honors the history and culture of Indigenous communities. It encourages us to reflect on how these groups have shaped the U.S. Corn, squash, and beans are traditionally important to the economic, cultural, and religious lives of many North American Indigenous communities. Indigenous people were the first to grow and develop these crops. Combine them with other ingredients to make a hearty yet refreshing salad!

Ingredients

¼ cup sugar
¼ cup white vinegar
2 tablespoons olive oil
1 cup zucchini, chopped
1 cup yellow squash, chopped
½ cup onion, chopped
½ cup green bell pepper, chopped
two 15-ounce cans black beans, drained and rinsed
two 15-ounce cans corn, drained and rinsed
cilantro for garnish (optional)

Supplies

knife and cutting board
strainer
measuring cups and spoons
saucepan
large bowl
spoon

1. Combine the sugar, vinegar, and olive oil in the saucepan to make dressing.

2. Heat the dressing on medium heat until it bubbles. Allow it to bubble for one minute. Then remove it from the heat and stir. Set the dressing aside to cool.

3. Put the zucchini, yellow squash, onion, bell pepper, beans, and corn into the bowl.

4. Pour the dressing into the bowl and stir to combine.

5. Chill the salad in the refrigerator until you are ready to serve it. If you'd like, garnish the salad with cilantro!

Food Fact!

Corn, beans, and squash are called the "Three Sisters" in some Indigenous communities. In these communities, Native people recognize that when the crops are planted close together, they help each other grow. They care for each other like sisters!

Spooky Pumpkins

Halloween is a time to dress up, eat sweets, and enjoy spooky decorations. Make these simple spooky pumpkins to become the hit of any Halloween party!

Ingredients

½ cup white chocolate chips
1 tablespoon vegetable oil
orange food coloring
24 chocolate sandwich cookies
green gummies
sugar eyes
black icing
white sprinkles

Supplies

measuring cups and spoons
microwave-safe bowl
spoon
spatula
parchment paper
baking sheet
knife and cutting board

1. Put the white chocolate chips and oil into the microwave-safe bowl. Microwave the chocolate in 20-second intervals, stirring between each one, until the chocolate is melted and smooth.

2. Stir eight drops of food coloring into the chocolate.

3. Spread the chocolate across the top of each cookie to make pumpkins.

4. Place the pumpkins onto the parchment-lined baking sheet.

5. Cut the green gummies into stem shapes. Place one on each pumpkin.

6. Place eyes on each pumpkin.

7. Use the icing to pipe mouths onto the pumpkins. Add sprinkles for teeth.

8. Place the baking sheet into the refrigerator so the chocolate sets. Serve your spooky pumpkins to friends and family!

Crisped Rice Turkeys

Thanksgiving is a holiday celebrating gratitude. It also marks the fall harvest. Turkey is a traditional Thanksgiving dish. Roasting a real turkey takes hours. But making these sweet treats only takes a few minutes!

Ingredients

3 tablespoons butter
5 cups mini marshmallows
6 cups crisped rice cereal
16-ounce can chocolate frosting
black icing
candy corn
malted milk balls
cashews, halved
red licorice

Supplies

knife and cutting board
measuring cups
microwave-safe bowl
spoon
parchment paper
baking sheet

1. Put the butter and mini marshmallows in the microwave-safe bowl. Microwave the mixture in 20-second intervals, stirring between each one, until the marshmallow is melted and smooth.

2. Stir the cereal into the marshmallow until the cereal is well coated.

3. Form the cereal mixture into balls. Flatten the bottoms to help them stand upright. Then place the balls onto the parchment-lined baking sheet. These are the turkeys' bodies.

4. Use the frosting to attach candy corns to the back of each turkey for a tail.

5. Use more frosting to attach a malted milk ball to each turkey's body for a head, a cashew half to each head for a beak, and a piece of licorice to each turkey's head for the snood.

6. Add eyes to the turkeys with the icing. Now you're ready to eat a full turkey in one big bite!

Reindeer Poop

Christmas is a holiday marked by twinkling lights, gift giving, and Santa Claus's flying reindeer. No matter how you celebrate Christmas, this silly treat is sure to make you laugh out loud!

Ingredients

½ cup butter
2 cups sugar
½ cup milk
¼ cup cocoa powder
½ cup peanut butter
2 teaspoons vanilla
½ teaspoon salt
3 cups quick oats

Supplies

measuring cups and spoons
saucepan
spatula
spoon
parchment paper
baking sheet

1. Heat the butter, sugar, milk, and cocoa powder in the saucepan on medium heat.
2. Stir the mixture occasionally until it boils. Let it boil for one minute and then remove it from heat.

3. Stir in the peanut butter, vanilla, and salt until smooth.
4. Add the oats to the mixture. Stir until they are coated.
5. Let the mixture cool and thicken for five minutes.
6. Spoon balls of the mixture onto the parchment-lined baking sheet.

7. Put the baking sheet in the refrigerator for five minutes to cool. Serve your "reindeer poop" to friends and family!

Spiced Meat Rolls

Eid al-Fitr is the feast that ends Ramadan, a month when Muslims fast. Some popular Eid al-Fitr dishes, such as samosa and kibbeh, feature crispy exteriors and spiced meat fillings. Have a little more than 15 minutes to cook? Then commemorate Eid al-Fitr with your own spiced meat rolls!

Ingredients

1 pound cooked, minced meat (plain ground beef or other)
1 cup milk
1 cup breadcrumbs
2 teaspoons cumin powder
1 teaspoon red chili powder
1 teaspoon garlic powder
2 teaspoons black pepper
1 teaspoon dried oregano
salt to taste
puff pastry sheet
1 egg

Supplies

measuring cups and spoons
mixing bowls
spoon
baking sheet
fork
basting brush
knife and cutting board

1. Preheat the oven to 400 degrees Fahrenheit (205 degrees Celsius).
2. Put the meat into a large mixing bowl. Add the milk and breadcrumbs, spices, and salt to the bowl. Mix well.
3. Roll out the puff pastry sheet.
4. Spoon the filling in a line down the center of the pastry.

5. Fold both long edges of pastry over the meat so they overlap, creating a roll.
6. Pinch the pastry edges together across the top and sides. Place the roll onto the baking sheet.

7. Crack the egg into a small mixing bowl. Whisk the egg with the fork to break the yolk. Brush the egg onto the top of the roll.
8. Bake the roll for 12 minutes.
9. Slice the roll into pieces after it has cooled. Then dig in!

Read More

Cardona, Dawn M. *Celebrate with Me! Recipes, Crafts, and Holiday Fun from around the World*. New York: Magic Cat, 2022.

Caswell, Mary Lou, and Deanna Caswell. *The Halloween Cookbook*. Mankato, MN: Black Rabbit Books, 2021.

Good Housekeeping. *1, 2, 3, Cook!* New York: Hearst Home Kids, 2022.

Internet Sites

11 Holiday Recipes from around the World
babbel.com/en/magazine/holiday-recipes-around-the-world

17 Holidays around the World
littlepassports.com/blog/world-holidays/holidays-around-the-world/

What's Your Favorite Holiday Cookie?
wonderopolis.org/wonder/What%E2%80%99s-Your-Favorite-Holiday-Cookie

About the Author

Tami grew up eating only peanut butter and jelly sandwiches and mac and cheese. It wasn't until she was an adult that food sparked her interest. Since then, she has thrown herself into trying new foods and improving every recipe she can find. She lives in Minnesota with her husband, two daughters, and a big orange cat.